GW00859245

Push and Pull

by Anne Giulieri

04462577

Here is my truck.

I can pull my truck.

3

I can push
my truck too.
It goes down the road.

Look at my door.

I can pull my door.

I can push my door too.

It shuts.

9

Here is my cart.

I can pull my cart.

My mum can
push my cart.
My cart goes
up and down.

Look at my swing.

My mum can push my swing.